BOSS MOVES

NO EXCUSES. JUST EXECUTION.

ADRIANA LUNA CARLOS

Editor-In-Chief, Designer
and Co-Founder

HANNA OLIVAS

Managing Editor &
Co-Founder

ADVERTISING OPPORTUNITIES

Info@SheRisesStudios.com

BOSS MOVES

JULY 2025

SHE RISES
STUDIOS

CONTACT US

editorial@sherisesstudios.com

WWW.SHERISESSTUDIOS.COM

LETTER FROM THE EDITORS

Dear Readers,

In the world of high-stakes entrepreneurship, it's easy to get caught in the momentum of scaling without stopping to ask—what am I building, and why does it matter? This month's edition of Boss Moves, "Scale With Purpose: The Legacy Edition," dives headfirst into that question, spotlighting founders who aren't just growing businesses—they're architecting impact, meaning, and long-term transformation.

At the helm of this conversation is our powerful cover feature, Michele Kline, a woman who has made it her mission to turn chaos into clarity and ambition into authentic leadership. As the founder of Kline Hospitality Consulting, Michele embodies what it means to lead with both precision and purpose. Her story is not only one of resilience and reinvention—it's a masterclass in legacy-building through people-centered strategy, emotional intelligence, and service-led leadership.

This edition isn't about hustle for hustle's sake. It's about alignment, intention, and the bold moves it takes to leave a footprint that outlasts the brand. Whether you're leading a team, launching a vision, or reinventing your role as a founder, the insights within these pages will challenge you to scale not just up—but deep.

Here's to building boldly, leading wisely, and moving with purpose.

Warm regards,

Adriana Luna Carlos and Hanna Olivas
Editors of Boss Moves Magazine

MICHELE KLINE

THE WOMAN WHO TURNS CHAOS INTO CLARITY

When you think of a boss making bold moves, breaking barriers, and transforming industries from the inside out, Michele Kline is that name. Not just a coach or a consultant, Michele is a powerhouse—an award-winning executive strategist, leadership visionary, and the founder of Kline Hospitality Consulting. But her success didn't happen by chance—it's the product of grit, heart, and a mission-driven mindset that refuses to settle for average leadership or disconnected culture.

Her brand? Transformation.
Her legacy? Impact.
Her method? Leading with heart, backed by science.

From Burnout to Breakthrough: The Making of a Leader

Before Michele Kline was coaching C-suite executives, reengineering company cultures, or helping international brands embrace hospitality as a leadership model, she was running herself into the ground in the name of performance. Years in high-level operations within the hospitality and service industry brought prestige—but also pressure. Like many ambitious women, she wore the stress like armor… until her body and mind said *"enough."*

"I didn't just burn out—I broke down," she recalls. *"I was living in a constant state of depletion.*

I was succeeding on paper but losing myself behind the scenes."

That pivotal moment became her turning point. Instead of staying stuck in a cycle of overwork and burnout, Michele leaned into transformation. She studied neuroscience, executive coaching, Total Quality Management, Six Sigma, Kaizen, and human behavior. And then—she rebuilt.

"I realized I didn't want to just lead operations anymore. I wanted to lead leaders."

Building a Boutique Empire

In 2010, Michele founded Kline Hospitality Consulting with one mission in mind: to move people from where they are to where they want to be. While initially focused on elevating leadership within the hospitality industry, her impact quickly expanded across tech, corporate, entertainment, public sector, and luxury retail brands. Why? Because her methods work—across industries, titles, and borders.

Kline Hospitality isn't your typical consulting firm. It's a transformation lab.

"We blend coaching, culture audits, leadership training,

and strategy—but at the core of everything is people. Businesses don't grow unless people grow."

The firm's services include brand standards audits, 360° leadership assessments, executive coaching, team dynamics workshops, and digital transformation partnerships. Her signature approach weaves together operational discipline and emotional intelligence—an often-missing combination in high-level leadership development.

360° Impact—And a Bestseller to Prove It

In 2024, Michele published her international bestselling book, *360° IMPACT: A Guide to Live, Lead, and Serve in a More Colorful World!* The book isn't just a leadership guide—it's a movement.

"My goal was to give people a practical, honest roadmap to lead with both purpose and performance," Michele says. *"I wanted it to feel like a toolbox, a pep talk, and a mirror all at once."*

In it, she breaks down the neuroscience of mindset, the science of high performance, and the heart-centered practices that make leaders memorable—not just effective.

It's no surprise that the book hit bestseller lists across multiple countries and led to the creation of *The 360° IMPACT Connection Labs*, a series of masterminds and retreats that empower leaders to connect deeply, communicate clearly, and lead courageously.

Walk the Floors: Leadership in Motion

True to her hands-on philosophy, Michele also co-hosts the award-winning podcast *WTF! Walk The Floors*—a bold call for leaders to get out from behind the desk and back into the heartbeat of service. In each episode, she tackles real workplace challenges, leadership blind spots, and the untold truths of managing people in fast-paced environments.

"We talk about the messy stuff—like the fact that most managers were promoted without being prepared to lead. And we remind leaders that proximity matters. You can't change what you won't walk through."

The podcast, which ranks in the Top 40 in global hospitality and business leadership categories, has cultivated a loyal following of leaders who are ready to roll up their sleeves and get real.

Championing the Next Generation

While Michele is a powerhouse in corporate rooms, she's just as passionate about reaching young people before burnout becomes a badge of honor. Through her *Champion Mindset* coaching for youth ages 11–17, she helps the next generation of leaders build confidence, resilience, and emotional agility.

"We're focused on changing outdated patterns as adults, without considering that we can equip young people with the mindset tools before the cracks even form."

It's just another example of Michele's signature style: lead forward, and always lead with purpose.

Recognition, Awards & Legacy

Michele's work hasn't gone unnoticed. Over the past several years, she's received an impressive lineup of accolades, including:
- Executive Coach of the Year – Global 100 (2023 & 2024)
- Most Transformative Leadership Coach – Global Excellence Awards
- Top 15 Coaches in Las Vegas – Influence Digest Media

- Top 25 Hospitality Executive to Watch – Global Hospitality Magazine
- Learning & Development Professional of the Year – Nevada Hotel & Lodging Association

But for Michele, the real reward is in the ripple effect.

"It's not about the title. It's about the impact. If I can help a leader feel seen, supported, and strong enough to show up for their team—that's legacy."

The Five Traits That Define Exceptional Leadership
According to Michele, what separates good leaders from exceptional ones isn't charisma or credentials. It's:

1. **Self-Awareness** – *"Exceptional leaders know who they are, what triggers them, and how to shift gears when needed."*
2. **Authentic Communication** – *"Say the thing. The kind, clear, direct thing."*
3. **Empathy** – *"This is a strategy, not a soft skill. Empathy builds trust, and trust builds results."*
4. **Adaptability** – *"The best leaders aren't rigid—they pivot with purpose, not panic."*
5. **Consistency** – *"Leadership isn't about moments. It's about showing up the same way when it's easy and when it's hard."*

What's Next?
Michele is currently expanding her firm's digital learning tools and planning international retreats for women in leadership. She's also working on her next book, diving deeper into redefining leadership beyond traditional corporate constructs.

"We're entering an era where people crave meaning, not just metrics. That's the future of leadership."

Final Thoughts: Boss Moves, the Michele Kline Way
What makes Michele Kline a true *Boss Moves* cover star isn't just her résumé—it's her relentless commitment to elevating the way we live, lead, and serve. Her career is proof that bold leadership isn't about power—it's about purpose. And real transformation doesn't come from perfect systems —it comes from perfectly human conversations.

So, if you're a leader looking to move from surviving to thriving, from high-performance to *whole-person* success— Michele Kline is the one you call.

Because in a world full of noise, her message rings clear:
You don't need to lead louder. You need to lead deeper.

Connect With Michele

www.klinehospitality.com
Podcast: WTF! Walk The Floors
Book: 360° IMPACT: A Guide to Live, Lead, and Serve in a More Colorful World!
IG: @micheleklinekhc
Linkedin: www.linkedin.com/in/micheleklinek/

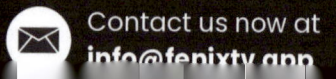

FENIX TV

YOUR PLATFORM, YOUR VOICE, YOUR POWER!

STEP INTO THE SPOTLIGHT AS A HOST ON FENIX TV!

Are you ready to amplify your message, inspire others, and be part of a groundbreaking network dedicated to empowering women worldwide? FENIX TV is your platform to shine as a host, share your expertise, and connect with a global audience.

WHY HOST ON FENIX TV?

- Reach a worldwide audience passionate about empowerment
- Showcase your voice, brand, and expertise
- Join a community of inspiring leaders and changemakers
- Be part of a network that uplifts and celebrates women

Whether you dream of leading a talk show, sharing powerful stories, or educating and inspiring others—FENIX TV is where your voice matters!

SECURE YOUR SPOT TODAY!

Contact us now at
info@fenixtv.app

Learn more at
https://fenixtv.app

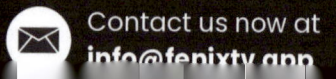
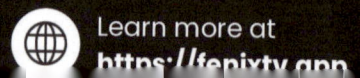

she wins

WOMEN'S NETWORK

Elevate your business with the power of community.

Get access to the tools, connections, and support you need to grow—with a circle of women who truly get it.

WHAT'S INCLUDED

- Strategic networking & mentorship
- Expert-led masterclasses & exclusive resources
- Member spotlights, VIP perks & more

Join for just

$87/MONTH

no contracts, cancel anytime.

www.shewinswomensnetwork.com

SHECONOMY™

A Global Economic Revolution Sparked by One Woman's Vision

By Adriana Luna Carlos | Co-Founder, She Rises Studios

When we talk about movements that change the world, we often picture a room full of policymakers, economists, or investors. But this one started with a woman—a mother, a leader, and a firestarter—who saw a future no one else was talking about.

Her name is Hanna Olivas, and she is the creator of The **Sheconomy™**.

This powerful term is more than a headline. It's a blueprint, a battle cry, and a worldwide movement designed to shift how money moves, how women lead, and how power is redistributed—permanently.

Hanna created The **Sheconomy™** out of necessity—because women are still asked to navigate systems that were never built for us. And instead of waiting for reform, she decided to lead a revolution.

What Is The Sheconomy™?

The **Sheconomy™** is Hanna's term for the unstoppable economic force that women already represent—and the system we must now build to match it.

It's not just about women entrepreneurs. It's about every woman—the single mother, the underpaid caretaker, the disabled worker, the immigrant leader, the first-generation graduate. It's about recognizing that women are the economy. And yet, we're still treated like we're asking for permission.

Women control over **$31.5 trillion** in global spending power. In the U.S. alone, nearly **40%** of businesses are owned by women. And women make **75%** of household purchasing decisions—from homes and healthcare to cars and technology.

So why are we still behind?

Because, as Hanna puts it: "We were never meant to thrive in systems we didn't build."

That's why she created The **Sheconomy™**—to change that permanently.

Why It Matters Now More Than Ever

The July 2025 **Sheconomy™** Report, written by Hanna and published in our She Rises Studios Newsletter, breaks down the urgent barriers that still hold women back. A few highlights:

- Only 2% of venture capital goes to women-led startups. Less than 1% goes to women of color.
- Women perform 2.5x more unpaid care work than men—a labor force that would add over $10 trillion to global GDP if compensated.
- In developing countries, over 45% of women entrepreneurs still lack affordable, reliable internet.
- Women globally have access to just 64% of the legal protections afforded to men.

These aren't just numbers. These are warning signs that we must address—because ignoring them keeps women trapped in cycles of invisibility and economic dependence.

Hanna's response? Build a system that makes us visible and powerful by design.

SHECONOMY ™

A Global Economic Revolution Sparked by One Woman's Vision

By Adriana Luna Carlos | Co-Founder, She Rises Studios

From Vision to Action

What makes Hanna's leadership different is that she didn't stop at defining the problem—she created the solution.

Under her guidance, She Rises Studios has launched The Sheconomy™ across multiple platforms, including:

- National and international events
- Books and publishing scholarships
- The Voices of 100 Women docuseries, now streaming in 127 countries on FENIX TV
- Workshops and online education
- Media campaigns reaching millions of women globally

And this is just the beginning.

Hanna believes that the only way to fix what's broken is to stop asking to be included—and start owning the table, the tools, and the rules. She often says, *"We don't need inclusion. We need ownership."*

The Sheconomy™ Is Not a Trend—It's the Future

Hanna's vision isn't just about making things better for women in business—it's about rewriting how we measure value altogether. That means:

- **Funding women relentlessly** at every level—from microloans to venture capital.
- **Closing the digital divide** so every woman has access to tools like AI, e-commerce, and automation.
- **Monetizing care work** and building national care infrastructures.
- **Normalizing women in power**—not as the exception, but the standard.

And above all, collaboration over competition. The Sheconomy™ thrives when women rise together—not alone, not in silence, and not in scarcity.

The July 2025 Sheconomy™ Report

You can read the full Sheconomy™ Report authored by Hanna Olivas through:

- **LinkedIn:** Follow Hanna Olivas for direct access
- **She Rises Studios Newsletter:** Subscribe at www.sherisesstudios.com

Inside, you'll find data-driven insights, global economic forecasts, and a practical roadmap for building the Sheconomy™ from the ground up.

Whether you're a founder, policymaker, educator, or woman simply trying to survive in today's economy—this report is for you.

Final Thoughts

It's rare that we get to watch history being made by someone we love, trust, and walk beside. I get to do that every day with Hanna. But make no mistake—what she has built with The Sheconomy™ belongs to every woman who's ever felt overlooked, underestimated, or underpaid.

This isn't just her vision. It's your future. It's our blueprint.

And it's already in motion.

So if you're wondering what comes next—look to The Sheconomy™.

Because women aren't waiting anymore.

We're building the world we deserve.

One woman. One vision. A global shift.

Let's build.

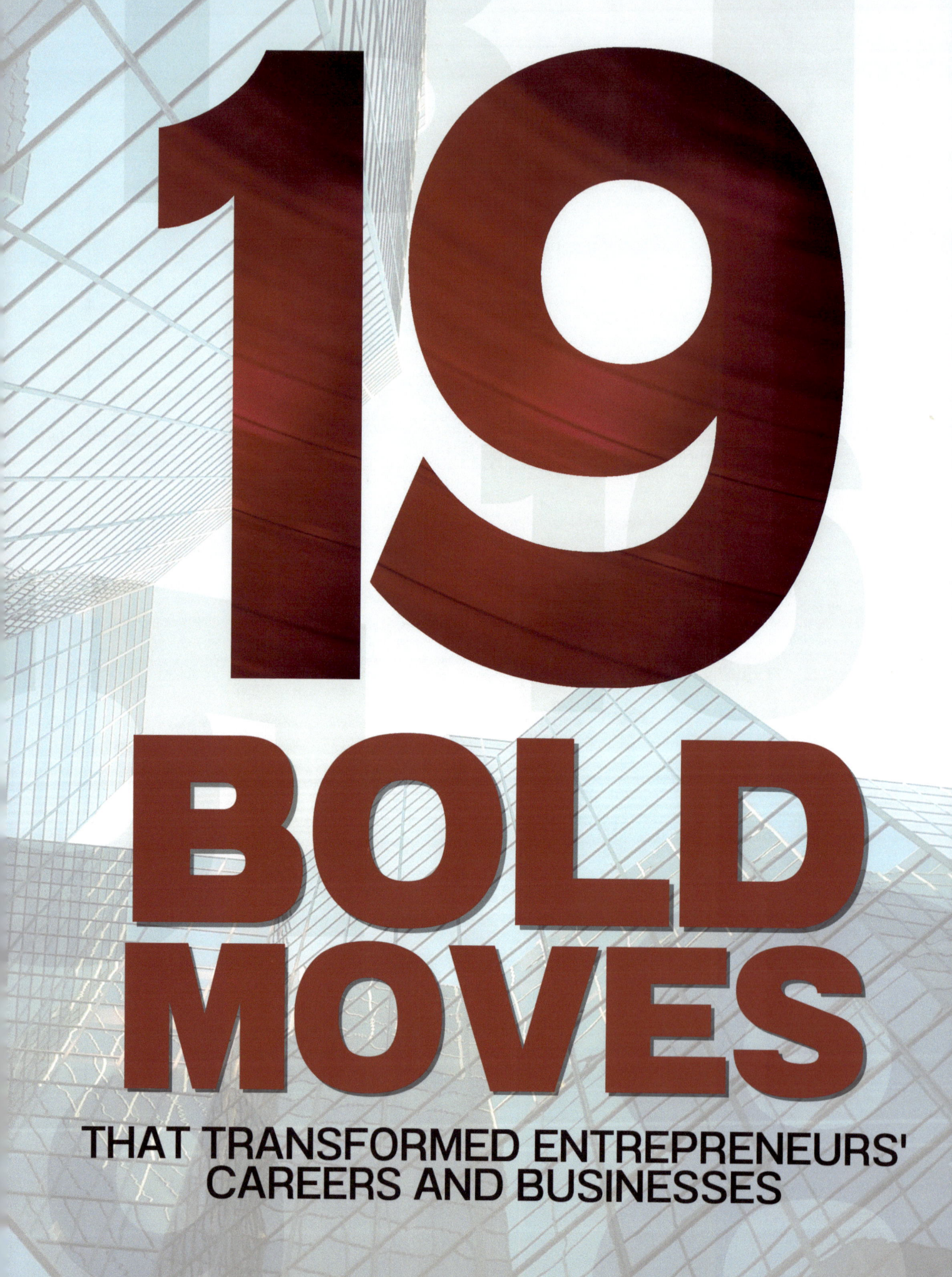

19
BOLD
MOVES

THAT TRANSFORMED ENTREPRENEURS' CAREERS AND BUSINESSES

ENTREPRENEUR BUILDS PET BRAND TO SAVE SHELTER ANIMALS

I'm a first-time entrepreneur, a first-generation immigrant, a woman, and a total outsider to the pet industry. But in late 2024, I put everything I had—my savings, my nights, my weekends—into launching a pet wellness brand with one mission: to reduce the number of animals surrendered to shelters and help more dogs get adopted faster.

The brand is called ShelterBaby.
(https://www.amazon.com/dp/B0D6V3NCW4)

I had no investors, no celebrity endorsements, and no business background. But I had years of shelter volunteering, and I kept seeing the same pattern: pets weren't surrendered because of a lack of love, but because of anxiety, skin problems, or health costs. I knew I could help solve that.

I spent over a year developing a dry coat care powder for dogs with allergies and chronic itch—using ingredients like astaxanthin, a luxury human skincare antioxidant that had never been used in pet products. I refused cheap fillers and committed to only organic, human-grade ingredients that support skin health and the microbiome.

I launched in one of the toughest categories on Amazon— pet care, a space dominated by influencers, legacy brands, and celebrity founders. I had none of that. But I had something they didn't: I believed in my product so much, I ate it on camera. Not for attention—but to prove how clean and safe it was.

And it worked. Within three months, we were profitable. ShelterBaby won the 2024 Pet Innovation Award for Best Bath Product—listed alongside industry giants like Zesty Paws and Pet Honesty. Our calming aid, developed for my own dog Beetlejuice, is now helping dogs in shelters feel safe enough to be adopted. That's what success looks like to me.

My advice? Don't wait until you feel ready. You don't need a perfect resume or a polished pitch. You need a problem worth solving, a reason bigger than fear, and the discipline to show up when no one's watching.

ShelterBaby was built from heartbreak and hope—and today, it's proof that when you lead with love and back it with science, dogs win.

Zhenya Villarreal, Founder, ShelterBaby

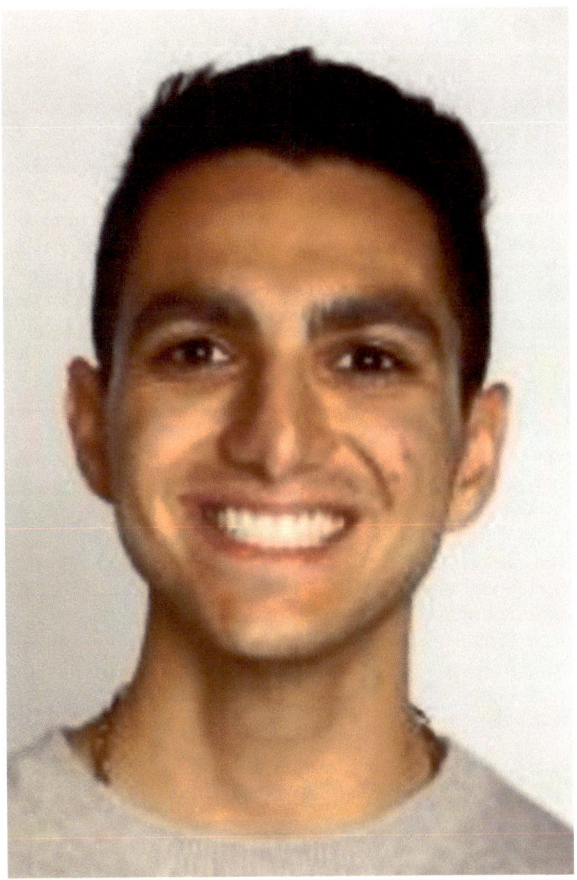

TEEN FARMER PIVOTS TO TECH WITH UNIQUE APPROACH

At 16, I was making decent money with Milan Farms, but I realized staying in agriculture would limit my long-term impact. Everyone thought I was crazy to walk away from profitable turtle breeding and farming to dive into the brutal world of tech startups in Silicon Valley.

I pivoted completely—shutting down my farming operations and founding Ankord Media with zero industry connections and a tiny budget. The first year was brutal; I was competing against established agencies with decades of experience while learning branding and design from scratch.

The breakthrough came when I started targeting early-stage startups instead of trying to win over big corporations. Our anthropologist-led user research approach helped a struggling fintech startup completely reposition their brand, leading to a successful Series A raise within 6 months. Word spread fast in the startup community.

My advice: don't compete where everyone else is fighting. Find the underserved niche where your unique perspective creates actual value. I learned that being young and inexperienced becomes an advantage when you're solving problems for other young founders who think differently than traditional businesses.

Milan Kordestani, *CEO, Ankord Media*

SOLAR COMPANY ABANDONS AI FOR JOURNALIST-FIRST STRATEGY

My defining moment came in early 2024 when I made the unapologetic decision to completely abandon our AI-generated content strategy at SunValue—despite having months of work and budget invested. While competitors were doubling down on automated content, I noticed our traffic becoming increasingly volatile after Google's algorithm updates.

I pivoted to what I called a *"journalist-first"* editorial model, blending expert interviews with local solar installation case studies. This meant higher costs, longer production times, and my team questioning whether we were moving backwards while others scaled with AI.

The change was dramatic. Within six months, our referring domains increased by 27% and our content started earning organic backlinks from major publications like Realtor.com without any outreach. Our *"Solar & Home Value"* collaboration with real estate analysts became one of the most shared pieces in our niche, generating 12 authoritative backlinks.

My advice: When everyone zigs, consider zagging—especially in oversaturated markets. The biggest opportunities often come from doing the opposite of what seems efficient. Sometimes the *"slower"* path creates defensible advantages that AI-first competitors can't replicate.

Nina Golban, *Search Engine Optimization Copywriter, SunValue*

MUSICIAN TRANSFORMS PODCAST INTO GLOBAL IP ASSET

My defining moment came three years into podcasting when I made the unapologetic decision to stop releasing music consistently and pour everything into the *"We Don't PLAY"* podcast. I had built my identity as *"Flaev Beatz"* for nearly 17 years, but the podcast was demanding my full attention to break through.

The numbers proved me right. We climbed from wherever we started to the top 2.5% of podcasts globally on ListenNotes, crossing 500 episodes and attracting guests from over 145 countries. This pivot opened doors I never imagined—international friendships, speaking opportunities on Clubhouse, and eventually scaling Work & PLAY Entertainment to a team of 21 people.

The real change happened when I realized podcasting wasn't just content creation—it was intellectual property asset building. Each episode became a building block for my digital marketing expertise, leading to sponsorship deals and our current podcast advertising packages that help other businesses grow beyond traditional sponsorship models.

My advice: Don't be afraid to put your established identity on pause for something with bigger potential. I learned that consistency in one focused direction beats scattered efforts across multiple projects. The hardest part was that year of mental preparation before launching, but that planning made all the difference when execution time came.

Favour Obasi-ike, *Project Scheduler, Work & PLAY Entertainment*

DATA STRATEGIST DISRUPTS MENTAL HEALTH TREATMENT MODEL

My career-defining moment came when I decided to leave my secure corporate strategy role to co-found Thrive Mental Health—despite having no direct clinical background and everyone questioning whether a "*data guy*" could lead a behavioral health company. The mental health crisis was exploding, but most providers were still using outdated models with terrible outcomes.

I invested everything into building a virtual IOP/PHP platform that combined clinical expertise with data-driven personalization. The risk was enormous—I was betting my reputation on an industry I didn't come from, during a time when virtual mental health was still stigmatized. But I saw the opportunity to bridge healthcare data analytics with behavioral health delivery.

The change was dramatic. Our evidence-based approach now delivers measurable results: clients show significant improvements in depression and anxiety symptoms, with 60% covered by Cigna alone. We scaled from zero to serving patients across Florida, South Carolina, and Indiana with our "Wellness First" culture reducing staff burnout by 35%.

My advice: Don't let industry gatekeepers convince you that outsider perspective is a weakness. The biggest breakthroughs often come from applying expertise from adjacent fields. I brought healthcare data strategy to behavioral health—what unique combination can you create? The intersection of your different experiences is where real innovation happens.

Nate Raine, *CEO, Thrive*

ENTREPRENEUR CREATES PREMIUM DRIVER SERVICE IN MEXICO

I put everything on the line in a private driver service in a city I didn't know — and it has changed my life.

In 2020, I sold my insurtech startup and moved to Mexico City thinking I'd fundraise for my next company; that didn't happen. COVID hit, all investors froze, and I found myself stuck in a foreign city — with no income, no plan, and no car.

But I had one idea: a premium private driver service for travelers and executives that needed trust, English-speaking support, and clarity on online booking, in a chaotic city. I was neither a local, nor did I know the market; I had zero logistics experience — but I went for it.

I built everything from scratch. I took/booked any calls or messages, responded to any WhatsApps, wrote all of the content, and hired every trusted driver through trial and error. I focused intensely on peace of mind: clear pricing based on routes, luggage information, confirmed pickup time — no surprise fees or last-minute steals. I even personally executed airport rescues at 2 am, multi-day wedding logistics, and dealt directly with a Fortune 100 CEO whose team requested succession vehicles and anonymity.

The growth has surprised even me. From clients requesting just a few rides a month, we quickly scaled to more than 70 requests; many from 5 star hotels and travel agents sending us directly. The average booking grew to $135 USD, and high end clients were spending more than $2,000 a week with us. Mexico-City-Private-Driver.com now shows up on Google for dozens and dozens of top search terms, not because I gamed it, but because I built something that people trust and talk about.

The biggest leap of faith, was not starting a business — it was gambling on service in a place where most people expect chaos. That decision — to lead with obsessive clarity and identify the human element — has changed everything.

My guidance to others, don't wait to be "*ready*". If a problem you see is real, and you care enough about the solution, do it. You don't need a fleet to start a transportation company. You don't need an entire map to build a company that people love. You just need to be relentless about building trust.

What I've created may not represent the largest fish in the city — but it is the most reliable fish for anyone who needs things done right. That is the kind of business that stands the test of time. And it all began with one significant risk, in a city that didn't know me — yet.

Martin Weidemann, *Owner, Mexico-City-Private-Driver.com*

SHOP NOW

Empowering Women through Wellness and Self-Care

SHE
glows

HANNA OLIVAS
Along With 26 Inspiring Authors

GRAB YOUR COPY NOW

SHE GLOWS: Empowering Women Through Wellness and Self-Care is a radiant collection of stories and strategies from women who've made wellness a priority—and transformed their lives in the process. Through real experiences, expert insights, and practical tools, this empowering book shows how self-care is not selfish, but essential. From mindfulness and movement to nutrition and boundary-setting, these stories remind us that true glow comes from within. You are not alone—and these women prove that healing, balance, and joy are all within reach when you choose to care for yourself first.

amazon.com   **SHE RISES** STUDIOS

GRAB YOUR COPY NOW

She Knows Her Worth: Empowerment through Self-Respect and Confidence is a heartfelt collection of stories from women who've faced self-doubt—and found their way to unshakable confidence. Through honest reflections and practical wisdom, these women share how they built boundaries, silenced inner critics, and learned to celebrate their worth. This empowering book is both a guide and a companion for anyone ready to embrace their true value and live boldly. You are not alone—and these stories are proof that confidence grows when you choose to honor your worth, every single day.

amazon.com   **SHE RISES** STUDIOS

FOUNDER SCRAPS FAVORITE FEATURE FOR INTERACTIVE DONOR WALL

My defining moment came when I decided to scrap our failing feature that I personally loved and bet everything on an interactive donor wall nobody was asking for. We were bleeding money at Rocket Alumni Solutions, and I had to choose between my ego and our survival.

I killed a product we'd spent months building and redirected our entire development budget toward touchscreen donor recognition displays. The risk was brutal—if this flopped, we were done. But I noticed schools kept mentioning how outdated their physical plaques looked, even though they weren't directly asking for digital solutions.

That pivot became our flagship product and drove us from near-bankruptcy to $3M+ ARR. The interactive displays increased repeat donations by 25% for our partner schools, and 40% of new donors at one school first heard about giving programs through our digital testimonials. We went from scrambling for survival to scaling nationwide.

My advice: Kill your darlings before they kill your business. The market doesn't care about your favorite features—it pays for solutions to problems people actually have. Sometimes the boldest move isn't building something new, but having the guts to destroy what isn't working and pivot everything toward what could work.

Chase Mckee, *Founder & CEO, Rocket Alumni Solutions - Digital Record Board*

HOST ABANDONS PROFITABLE PROPERTIES TO PROTECT GUEST EXPERIENCE

My defining moment came when I had to make the brutal decision to walk away from two profitable Airbnb properties simultaneously—one where the landlord was poaching my guests, another where the downstairs neighbor was harassing them with loud music and confrontations. I was losing money daily but knew guest safety trumped everything.

Instead of trying to salvage bad situations, I cut ties immediately and relocated both operations within two weeks. This meant eating security deposits, moving costs, and temporary revenue loss while scrambling to find better properties. The financial hit was painful, but I refused to compromise on guest experience.

The results transformed my entire business model. Guest satisfaction scores jumped from 4.2 to 4.8 stars, repeat bookings increased 30%, and I developed a rigorous landlord/neighbor vetting process that's prevented similar issues since. More importantly, I learned that protecting your brand reputation is worth more than any single profitable property.

My advice: When your gut tells you a situation is toxic, act fast and cut losses rather than trying to manage dysfunction. In hospitality, one bad experience creates ten negative reviews, but one great experience creates loyal customers who book repeatedly and refer others.

Sean Swain, *Company Owner, Detroit Furnished Rentals LLC*

FINANCE PROFESSIONAL BUILDS SKILLS-FIRST HIRING PLATFORM

In 2016, I walked away from a stable corporate job in finance to launch a startup in an industry I'd never worked in: recruitment tech. Everyone thought I was out of my mind including me, at times. I didn't have a background in HR or SaaS. What I did have was a front-row seat to how broken and biased hiring systems could be, and an idea for how to fix them.

The turning point came after watching yet another talented candidate get rejected based on a resume instead of their real skills. I realized the problem wasn't the people, it was the process. I didn't want to just complain about it. I wanted to rebuild it.

So I took the risk. I left my job. I invested my own money. I started from zero.

The first year was brutal. I wasn't a tech founder by trade, and I made all the early mistakes: overbuilding features, targeting the wrong customers, hiring too fast. But I kept learning, kept testing, and most importantly, kept listening. Listening to recruiters, to candidates, to hiring managers who were just as frustrated as I was.

That's how Testlify was born, an AI-powered skills assessment platform designed to help companies hire for what actually matters: ability, not pedigree. And when our first customers told us it was saving them hours of work and helping them find better-fit candidates, I knew we were on the right path.

Fast forward to today: Testlify is used by companies in over 50 countries. We've grown to a team of 80+, hit $1M+ ARR, and helped hundreds of teams make more confident, fairer hiring decisions.

But the biggest win isn't the revenue, it's knowing we built something real, from scratch, that solves a real problem.

What I learned: The boldest move you'll ever make is betting on yourself. Especially when there's no blueprint. Especially when no one else sees it yet.

People often wait for the "*perfect time*" to make their big move. But here's the truth: bold moves are never comfortable. If it feels safe, it's probably not bold enough.

My advice to others: You don't need to have it all figured out. You just need to believe that your reason is stronger than your fear. Start where you are. Learn as you go. And don't let imposter syndrome keep you from building the thing only you can build.

Abhishek Shah, *Founder, Testlify*

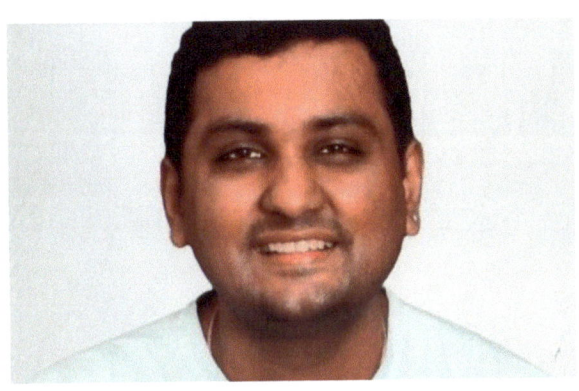

AGENCY TRANSFORMS CANNABIS MARKETING WITH MOBILE GAMING VAN

My biggest risk came when advertising restrictions hit our cannabis clients hard in 2019—platforms were banning accounts left and right, and traditional paid ads became nearly impossible. Instead of playing it safe with compliant digital tactics, I convinced my team to invest everything into physical experiential marketing with a branded mobile gaming van.

We bought a Sprinter van, loaded it with gaming setups, and started parking outside dispensaries and high-traffic areas. People could play NBA 2K and Mario Kart, then redeem in-store promotions. My team thought I'd lost it—we were a digital agency pivoting to what looked like a food truck operation.

That mobile tour became our signature offering and drove 20% increases in first-time customers at every location we visited. The organic social content from people filming themselves gaming in our van went viral multiple times, and we landed five new six-figure clients who specifically wanted our "*van strategy.*" Revenue jumped 180% that year.

The lesson: When your industry's rules change overnight, don't just adapt—completely reimagine what's possible. My advice for bold moves is to look at what everyone else considers impossible due to regulations or limitations, then find the gap where creativity meets compliance. Sometimes the biggest opportunities hide behind the biggest restrictions.

Stephen Gold, *Business Owner, The Gold Standard*

FORMER CONVICT OPENS SUCCESSFUL QUEENS CANNABIS DISPENSARY

The moment that transformed everything: When New York's CAURD program launched, I had to choose between my stable construction career and pursuing the first legal dispensary license in Astoria. Everyone thought I was crazy —a guy with multiple cannabis convictions trying to go legitimate in an industry that barely existed yet.

I liquidated my safety consulting business and invested every dollar into Terp Bros, despite having zero retail experience. The licensing process alone took 18 months with no guaranteed outcome. I was betting my entire future on a program designed for people like me, but the failure rate was brutal.

The change was immediate and massive. Within six months of opening, we became the go-to dispensary in Queens. We were one of the first to carry Issa Vibe products when Nargis Hakimi launched her brand—those vape pens became our bestsellers with new customers. Our community-focused approach drove word-of-mouth so hard that we're now expanding to a second location in Ozone Park.

My advice: Your biggest liability can become your greatest asset. My criminal record was supposed to disqualify me from business success, but it became the exact qualification needed for CAURD. Don't let others define what's possible for you—especially when new industries are forming. The people who win are the ones willing to risk everything when the rules are still being written.

Jeremy Rivera, *CEO, Terp Bros*

JUSTICE SYSTEM BACKGROUND BECOMES DISPENSARY'S COMPETITIVE EDGE

My defining moment came when I decided to open Kaya Bliss Dispensary in Southern Brooklyn with my business partner Giorgio—despite having a background in the justice system that many would see as a liability in the cannabis industry. Everyone told us to downplay that history, but I made the unapologetic decision to make it central to our brand story and mission.

I leveraged my personal journey with the justice system as our unique selling proposition, emphasizing social equity and community empowerment rather than hiding it. We built our entire recruitment and marketing strategy around creating opportunities for marginalized communities and being transparent about our commitment to giving back. This attracted local influencers, business leaders, and top talent who connected with our mission.

The change was immediate—our transparency about social equity set us apart from every other dispensary in Brooklyn. Before we even opened, we had a loyal following and strong partnerships with local businesses. When construction delays hit, our community-first approach kept customers engaged through virtual events and collaborations, creating massive buzz for our eventual opening.

My advice: Your perceived weaknesses can become your greatest strengths if you own them completely. The cannabis industry is full of corporate players trying to sanitize their image—we went the opposite direction and made our authentic story our competitive advantage. Don't let others define what qualifies you for success.

Edgar Kleydman, *Founding Member, Kaya Bliss Dispensary*

BROKER CREATES AI TOOL FOR COMMERCIAL REAL ESTATE

My defining moment came when I decided to build a proprietary AI deal analyzer for commercial real estate in Miami—despite having zero tech background and everyone telling me AI was just hype. I was tired of spending 6 hours manually creating market reports and watching deals slip away because we couldn't analyze lease terms fast enough.

I invested $50K of my own money and six months learning to work with developers to create our AI platform. The risk was massive—I could have lost everything and looked like an idiot chasing tech trends in a traditional industry. But I knew data-driven decisions would separate winners from losers in CRE.

The change was immediate. Our AI tool cut my market report writing from 6 hours to 90 minutes with 80% fewer manual errors. More importantly, it flagged a rental rate spike in Northwest Doral six months before CoStar reported it publicly—I helped three clients renew early and saved them over $200K collectively. Our tenant-side renewals jumped 35% and negotiation cycles shortened from 45 to 28 days.

My advice: Don't wait for permission to innovate in traditional industries. Most of our $2M+ in client savings came from that one bold tech investment. The biggest risk isn't failing—it's staying comfortable while your industry evolves without you.

Brett Sherman, *Real Estate Broker, Signature Realty*

SALES LEADER BUILDS AUTOMATION SYSTEMS FOR LOCAL BUSINESSES

My defining moment came when I walked away from a stable 20-year career leading B2B sales teams to start Growth Catalyst Crew. Everyone thought I was crazy leaving guaranteed income to help "*small local businesses with digital marketing.*"

The pivot happened when I realized most agencies were charging premium prices for cookie-cutter solutions that didn't work for local service businesses. I bet everything on building proprietary AI systems and automation that could deliver measurable results—like 40%+ response rates on follow-up sequences when industry average was 15%.

Within 90 days, our first electrician client in Augusta saw 80% organic traffic growth and consistent job bookings. Our healthcare client broke past 50 reviews (stuck there for 3 years) to over 200 reviews in 12 months, hitting top 3 Google Maps visibility.

The real breakthrough was proving that automation doesn't have to be impersonal. While competitors were selling expensive retainer packages, we built systems that actually worked—like helping clients collect 100+ Google reviews without gimmicks or getting 51% email open rates with seasonal campaigns. My advice: Don't just solve problems differently—solve problems others won't touch because they seem too specific or small-scale.

Raymond Strippy, *Founder, Growth Catalyst Crew*

GRAB YOUR COPY NOW

Her Path to Entrepreneurship: A Journey of Courage, Vision, and Success shares the real, unfiltered stories of women who turned ambition into action—and built thriving businesses on their own terms. From startup struggles to leadership wins, these powerful journeys offer insight, strategy, and the motivation to keep going. Whether you're just beginning or growing your next big idea, this collection proves that success comes in many forms—and every path is worth celebrating. You are not alone—and these stories show that with courage and vision, anything is possible.

amazon.com   **SHE RISES** STUDIOS

COACH LAUNCHES UNMANNED 24/7 BASEBALL TRAINING FACILITY

My career-defining moment was opening MVP Cages as a 24/7 unmanned facility when everyone told me it was too risky. Coming from coaching youth baseball, I was frustrated watching families drive 45 minutes for mediocre cage time that closed at 8 PM.

I invested everything into keycode access systems, surveillance tech, and automated waivers—basically betting my family's future on parents trusting an unstaffed facility with their kids. The liability concerns kept me up at night, but I knew flexibility was what baseball families desperately needed.

Within six months, we hit profitability and doubled our customer base. Parents loved booking 6 AM sessions before school or 10 PM after games. Our retention rate jumped to 85% because families could finally train on their schedule, not ours.

The real game-changer was pre-selling memberships before we opened. Instead of taking loans, I sold $15,000 in credits during construction, which covered startup costs and gave us a built-in client base on day one.

My advice: Don't ask for permission to solve a problem you know exists. Most "*traditional*" business owners in youth sports told me unmanned facilities would never work—meanwhile, we're booked solid while staffed competitors struggle with overhead. Trust your instincts over industry veterans who profit from keeping things complicated.

Steve Sliker, *Owner, MVP Batting Cages*

CONSULTANT BUILDS INDEPENDENT RENEWABLE ENERGY NEWS PLATFORM

My defining moment came when I decided to pivot from traditional renewable energy consulting to launching MicroGridMedia.com as a dedicated news platform. Everyone questioned why I'd leave stable consulting work to enter the crowded media space, but I saw a massive gap in quality renewable energy journalism that wasn't just press releases.

I invested my savings into building a proper newsroom infrastructure and hiring experienced journalists like Andrew, who covers the intersection of energy technology and political economy. The risk was enormous—media is notoriously difficult to monetize, and I was competing against established energy publications with decades of history.

The change was remarkable. Within months, we became the go-to source for breaking renewable energy stories, from covering Jaguar Land Rover's "*Lighting Up Lives*" initiative reaching 1.2 million off-grid East Africans to analyzing major industry bankruptcies like SunPower's recent filing. Our readership grew exponentially because we provided actionable insights instead of surface-level reporting.

My advice: Find the information gap in your industry that everyone complains about but no one fixes. Don't just create another business—solve the problem that keeps your target audience frustrated. The companies that win are the ones filling genuine knowledge voids, not adding to the noise.

Jonas Muthoni, *Editor in Chief, MicroGrid Media*

MARKETER REBUILDS AGENCY AROUND AI AUTOMATION SYSTEMS

My defining moment came when I decided to completely shut down my existing marketing operations and rebuild everything around AI automation—while still serving existing clients. Everyone thought I was crazy to risk a profitable business model, but I saw traditional marketing agencies drowning in manual work while charging clients for inefficient processes.

I invested heavily in AI tools and rebuilt our entire service delivery from scratch. Instead of having teams spend 8 hours creating social media campaigns, we trained AI systems to handle content creation, optimization, and scheduling in under 2 hours. The risk was massive—if it failed, I'd lose clients and waste months of development time.

The change was immediate and dramatic. Our client delivery speed increased 300% while maintaining quality, allowing us to take on more clients without expanding our team proportionally. One law firm client saw their website inquiries jump 40% after we implemented our new AI-optimized web design process, and a local business literally doubled their sales in 3 months using our streamlined approach.

My advice: Don't just adopt new technology—completely reimagine your business model around it. Most entrepreneurs try to patch AI onto existing processes instead of rebuilding from the ground up. The companies winning right now aren't the ones using AI as a side tool, they're the ones who made AI the foundation of how they operate.

Seth Gillen, *Owner, Sierra Exclusive Marketing*

NEW HIRE VOLUNTEERS FOR BILLION-DOLLAR REBRANDING PROJECT

My career-defining moment happened five months into my first corporate job when I raised my hand to lead a billion-dollar company's complete rebranding project. Everyone thought I was crazy—I was the newest hire with zero corporate experience volunteering for their highest-stakes marketing initiative.

The risk paid off massively. The rebranding project's success catapulted me directly into a Director role overseeing special projects, skipping years of traditional career ladder climbing. More importantly, it taught me my superpower: taking fluid ideas and creating concrete execution roadmaps that actually work.

This experience shaped how I approach my current role at Chike Nutrition. When I joined as Brand and E-commerce Manager, I applied the same "*raise your hand first, figure it out second*" mentality to revolutionize how we tell customer stories and connect with our health-conscious audience.

My advice: Volunteer for the project everyone else is avoiding, especially early in your career. The combination of high visibility and low expectations creates the perfect storm for massive upside. I learned that companies desperately need people who can bridge the gap between big ideas and practical implementation—and they'll reward you handsomely for it.

Mac Mascorro, *Director of Marketing, Chike*

JOURNALIST CREATES INDEPENDENT ENTERTAINMENT NEWS PUBLICATION

My defining moment came when I launched The Showbiz Journal as an independent outlet after working within corporate-controlled media structures. Everyone warned me that entertainment journalism was oversaturated and that going independent meant losing stable income and industry access.

I took the leap anyway, investing my savings into building a publication that could cover stories authentically without corporate interference. The risk was massive—I was competing against established outlets with massive budgets while bootstrapping everything from content creation to SEO strategy.

The change happened faster than expected. Within months, our authentic coverage of celebrity stories like Rebel Wilson's empowerment journey and industry strikes resonated with readers craving genuine perspectives.

Our traffic grew consistently because we weren't afraid to tackle complex topics like AI's impact on Hollywood or spotlight emerging entrepreneurs like Tanya Jane.

The key insight: audiences can smell authenticity from miles away. When you're not filtering stories through corporate agendas, your voice becomes distinctive. My advice is to identify what makes your perspective unique and double down on it, even if it means starting smaller. Independence might seem riskier, but creative freedom often leads to breakthrough content that stands out in crowded markets.

Jonas Muthoni TSJ, *Editor, The Showbiz Journal*

SHE RISES
S T U D I O S

JOIN THE SRS COMMUNITY

WHERE WOMEN RISE TOGETHER!

Connect. Empower. Thrive. Whether you're an entrepreneur, professional, or simply seeking inspiration, **this is your space to grow!**

- Daily Motivation
- Expert Insights
- Sisterhood & Support

You don't have to do it alone—let's rise together!

JOIN NOW!

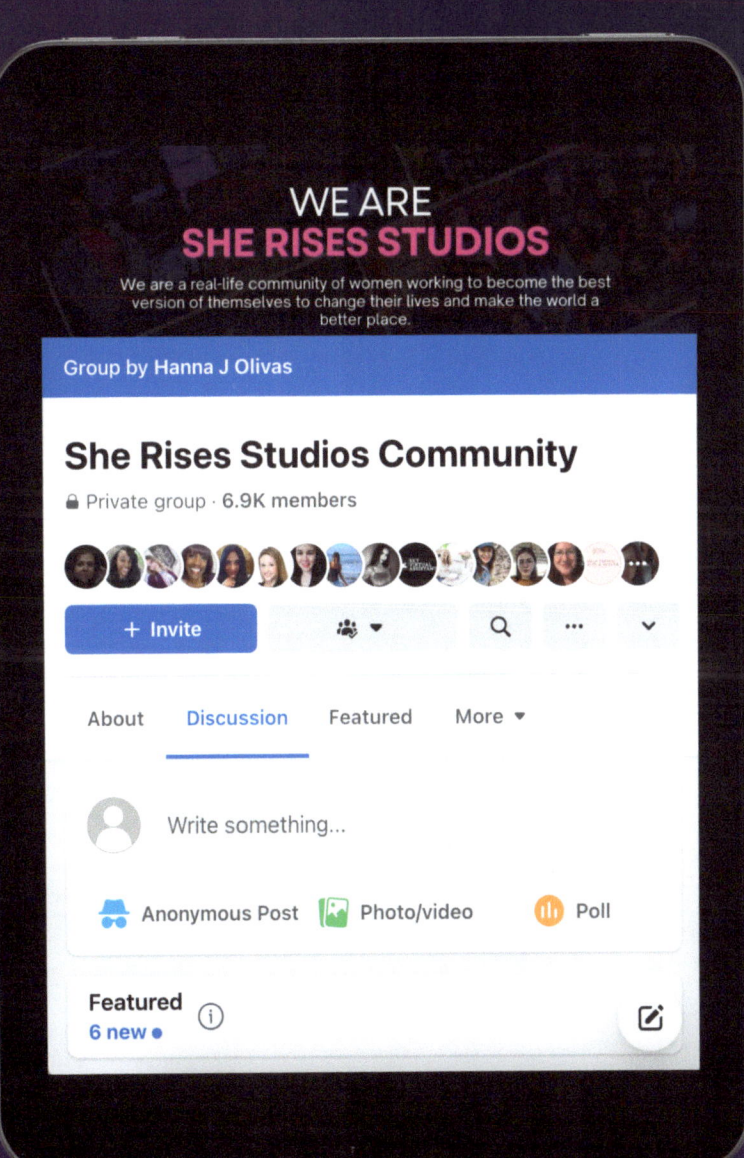

FROM OVERWHELMED TO EMPOWERED:

TRANSFORMING A FAMILY'S STRUGGLE WITH ANXIETY INTO A MOVEMENT FOR HEALING

By **Liz Prybylo**
Founder of Confident Kids Club

There wasn't one big, dramatic moment that set me on my current path. Instead, it was a slow culmination of moments that brought clarity —a journey that started with my child's worsening anxiety.

At first, the worries seemed manageable. But as my son's generalized anxiety and OCD grew stronger, daily life became harder. School became impossible, and eventually, we had to keep him home.

Every single day of my life felt like I had to suit up for battle —managing behaviors, meltdowns, and the inability to get through basic daily tasks. What followed was a long, exhausting stretch: nine months to get him evaluated, many more months to find a counselor he connected with, and over a year in therapy before we started to see meaningful progress. Through it all, I felt stuck—desperate to help, but unsure how.

I did what so many parents in that situation do. I read, I researched, I tried every well-meaning suggestion I could find. And slowly, I started to learn. I learned what helped and what didn't. I learned how to be steady for him, how to create small, safe steps forward, and how to help him feel capable in the face of his fears. But more than anything, I learned how hard it is for parents to know where to start when anxiety takes over their child's life.

That experience shifted something in me. I realized I didn't just want to figure it out for my own family—I wanted to be part of making the process better for others. I wanted to help parents and kids feel supported sooner, to make the tools for handling anxiety feel approachable, playful, and progressive. I wanted families to feel like they could learn together how to face anxiety with strategies that were grounded in research, not just guesswork.

That's when it became clear to me that my next step needed to combine two things: psychology and entrepreneurship. I knew I wanted to work toward becoming a school counselor so I could be part of supporting children and families directly. And I knew I wanted to build resources that could give families practical, engaging ways to build skills at home— resources I wish I'd had during those long months of waiting and wondering how to help.

That realization has shaped everything I've done since. I returned to graduate school to earn my Master of Education in School Counseling. I wanted the knowledge and training to back up my lived experience with professional expertise. And I began developing ideas that eventually became Confident Kids Club, a business focused on creating screen-free, play-based tools to help families support their children's emotional health. The work I do now is driven by that same purpose: to help children and families feel more confident, more connected, and more capable in facing anxiety.

That journey taught me that leadership doesn't always come from having the answers right away. Sometimes, it comes from living the questions, and choosing to turn hard-won lessons into something that helps others. That's what drives me now. And that's the kind of leader I strive to be every day.

Connect With Liz

www.confidentkidboxes.com
Instagram & Facebook:
@ConfidentKidsHQ

FROM SILENCE TO STRENGTH:

HOW ONE DEFINING MORNING SPARKED A MISSION TO AMPLIFY VOICES THAT MATTER

By **Amanda Zantal-Wiener**
Founder & Managing Partner of
Butcher, Baker, Beatmaker

One morning, my boss publicly berated me in front of my colleagues, dismissing weeks of painstaking work, dedication, and strategic planning.

The shift seemed sudden, but familiar. Up until that week, he had pretended to be my friend. Sure, I knew better. I'd seen this movie before. And after spending more years than I'd like to admit answering to managers like him, it was far from the first time I'd observed or endured this toxic cycle of praise followed swiftly by humiliation. But something about this day felt different. Conclusive. Weirdly illuminating.

Despite knowing better, I still spent time that day questioning my professional choices. And for whatever reason, that thought spiral parlayed into documenting everything: every insult, every act of intimidation, and every undermining tactic. It was cathartic, but infuriating, especially as I started to notice a pattern: I was fighting battles that didn't matter. They were the battles of corporate toxicity, and not the good fight that aligned with my purpose and values.

I wasn't meant to be doing this, to use my years of experience to help improve a corporation's valuation. I was meant to use my skills to empower those whose stories deserve to be heard. I was meant to amplify voices that push boundaries, reclaim narratives, and drive meaningful change through authentic storytelling and creative courage.

The very next day, after just six and a half weeks of being retained by this company, I was called into a meeting to learn that my role was being eliminated. Ah, yes. There was the illuminating finality. The choice was made for me. Continuing to invest my skills, passion, and energy into an endless capitalist churn, where impact mattered less than profit margins, was a complete misuse of my energy.

Today, I'm committed to building something radically different: an entity rooted in creative expression, integrity, and inclusivity. I founded Butcher, Baker, Beatmaker, dedicating myself to projects that honor diverse voices, genuine stories, and artistic courage. And today, that defining moment guides every decision I make as a leader.

Silently enduring verbal abuse at the hands of corporate leaders serves no one. A lot of silence serves no one. Instead, I've realized, amplifying the stories and voices that matter is a responsibility. It's my calling, not my choice.

That one particular morning, which was somehow simultaneously harrowing, illuminating, confusing, and enlightening, endures. It drives me to pursue and champion bold storytelling rooted in authenticity and humanity. I practice listening first, with a promise to lead with empathy, strength, and an unwavering commitment to creating environments where no one ever feels voiceless, erased, or dismissed.

Connect With Amanda

www.utcherbakerbeatmaker.com
www.amandazw.com
www.linkedin.com/in/amandazantalwiener

BOLD RISK REPLY

By **Amanda Duff, M.S., SHRM-CP**
Certified Coach | HR Consultant | Leadership Advisor

The boldest move I ever made was walking away from the stable, well-paying job I had built over a decade, with people I genuinely liked, to take a role that had an expiration date.

At the time, I was an HR Director making six figures, working with people I'd known for years. I was respected, trusted, and comfortable. But I wasn't passionate about the work anymore. I knew I could keep coasting along, but something in me had shifted. I wanted to build something of my own. I wanted to coach, consult, lead, but on my own terms. And I knew I'd never do it if I stayed comfortable.

So when an opportunity came up at a smaller company on the path to acquisition, I took it. I knew the role would end eventually. It was part of the deal. But I also saw it as a runway: a chance to help a company through a major transition and give myself the space to get ready for what I knew was next.

I negotiated a severance package before I even accepted the offer. That was my safety net, and my deadline. When the company got acquired, I'd be out of a job. But I'd also be free. Free to finally launch my business.

People thought I was a little nuts. Leaving a secure job you've had for 10 years for something unstable, with an end date, on purpose? But I knew I couldn't keep putting off what I really wanted. I needed the push. I needed the risk.

And honestly? It was scary. That in-between time, knowing this job would end, not yet running my own thing full-time, was full of imposter syndrome and second-guessing. But I also got to sharpen my skills, expand my experience, and make the connections that would carry me into the next chapter.

And when the day finally came, and I walked out of that job knowing I was officially on my own? It was terrifying.. and exhilarating.

Now, I run my own coaching and consulting practice. I help high-achieving professionals figure out what's next when they're tired of playing by someone else's rules. I help organizations build people-first HR strategies that actually support the humans who work there. I do work I care deeply about, and I've built it in a way that aligns with how I want to live and lead.

That bold move, leaving comfort for possibility, changed everything.

What I've learned: If you wait until you're 100% ready, you'll never go. Leaving something good in search of something better always feels risky. But sometimes, that leap is the only way forward.

So if you're sitting in a job that looks fine on the outside but feels empty on the inside.. trust that. You don't need to blow everything up overnight. But you can start making moves toward the future you actually want.

Comfort is safe, but it can also be a trap. I had to give up stability to make space for something better. And it worked.

Founder of a boutique coaching and consulting practice helping high-achieving professionals and small business leaders build more sustainable, human-centered ways of working.

Connect With Amanda

www.nowwhathr.com
@nowwhathr

BURN THE PLAN, BUILD THE FUTURE:
ONE FOUNDER'S REMOTE WORK REVOLUTION

By **Dr. Milly Barker**
Founder of RemotePad

I am Milly Barker, a Tech Entrepreneur and Founder of RemotePad (***https://remotepad.net/***). I have over 8 years of experience in startup operations and business pivots. I would love to share my bold move story.

Situation: Back in 2019, RemotePad was struggling as a traditional recruitment platform. We were bleeding money, barely keeping up with competitors, and I was honestly ready to shut down. The pandemic hit, and remote work exploded, but we weren't positioned to capitalize on it.

Move: I made what everyone thought was a crazy decision, and I pivoted our entire business model overnight. Instead of competing in the crowded recruitment space, I bet everything on becoming a remote work infrastructure company. We went from helping companies find talent to helping them manage distributed teams.

We scrapped 70% of our existing code, laid off half our team, and rebuilt from scratch in 4 months. I burned through my savings and took on debt to make it happen.

That pivot changed everything. Revenue jumped 340% in our first year post-pivot.

What mattered, though, we found our purpose. Instead of being another job board, we were endowing businesses with the tools to thrive remotely.

The entrepreneurs winning right now are making bold bets on where the world's heading.

Regards,
Milly Barker
Founder of RemotePad
camilla@remotepad.com
Profile: *https://remotepad.net/author/milly/*

Connect With Milly

www.remotepad.net

INSPIRE
EMPOWER
EDUCATE

GRAB YOUR COPY NOW

EmpowerHER: Narratives Rooted in Truth, Driven by Resilience, and Led by Women is a raw and powerful collection of real stories from women who've faced life's deepest hardships—and found strength on the other side. From illness and loss to trauma and recovery, these honest journeys reveal the power of resilience, healing, and inner transformation. More than survival, these stories show what it means to rise with purpose and lead with truth. You are not alone—and these women prove that even in the darkest moments, there is always a way forward, and always a reason to keep rising.

LISA STAMPER

THE INTUITIVE ARCHITECT OF EMPIRE-BUILDING

Power. Wealth. Alignment. Legacy. Few leaders embody these principles as wholly and powerfully as Lisa Stamper.

A visionary, a strategist, and a soul-led mentor to high-achieving women, Lisa Stamper is making legendary moves in the entrepreneurial space—and she's doing it without compromise.

As a 7-figure creator, high-ticket mentor, and intuitive business expert, Lisa is guiding the next wave of founders, CEOs, and thought leaders to build legacy-level empires rooted in energetic mastery, financial sovereignty, and unshakable self-trust. Her unique ability to blend aligned strategy with spiritual depth has earned her a global reputation as the go-to mentor for women ready to scale with power and purpose.

Lisa is the founder of the Evolve Community, the creator of the transformational L.E.T. Method™ and The Millionaire Flow Protocol©, and the bestselling author of The Success Codes—a trailblazing book that deconstructs traditional definitions of success and helps readers unlock the wealth and power already within them. Ranked #5 on BookAuthority's list of *"20 Best New Success Books to Read in 2024"* and spotlighted on Times Square's iconic digital billboards, The Success Codes is more than a book—it's a call to liberation.

And that's exactly what Lisa delivers: liberation from the limiting beliefs, outdated models, and burnout-driven blueprints that keep powerful women playing small.

A New Paradigm for Scaling

Lisa's ethos is clear: hustle is outdated. What works now is alignment.

In a landscape where many business mentors preach grind culture and rigid frameworks, Lisa's teachings come from a different frequency—one of inner knowing, embodiment, and flow. Her programs are not about following someone else's roadmap. They're about calibrating to your own brilliance and unlocking quantum-level expansion that's both sustainable and deeply fulfilling.

"Everything changes when you stop building from pressure and start building from power," Lisa shares. *"When your strategy is aligned with your soul, growth becomes inevitable."*

Her clients—many of whom are scaling past six and seven figures—don't just increase revenue. They shift identities. They claim space. They master their message, elevate their brand presence, and design offers that feel like home to their audience and their higher selves.

Through high-level mentorship containers, intensives, and luxury immersions, Lisa teaches high-performing women how to activate their leadership frequency and hold greater levels of wealth, visibility, and influence. And she walks her talk—having scaled her own empire in integrity, without sacrificing time, peace, or purpose.

Built for Bold Moves

Lisa's presence in the business world is nothing short of magnetic. She's shared the stage with icons like Jack Canfield and Deepak Chopra, and has spoken at elite institutions including Harvard, UCLA, Stanford, Oxford, and Cambridge. Her thought leadership bridges the spiritual and the strategic—an intersection she believes is key to building legacies that last.

"Too many leaders are stuck in one polarity—either all strategy or all spirit," Lisa says. *"True mastery comes when you integrate both. That's when you become unstoppable."*

Lisa's genius lies in this integration. She's an intuitive channel with decades of spiritual practice—and a world-class strategist who understands high-converting systems, scalable offers, and sustainable growth models. This rare blend positions her as a next-level mentor in a noisy industry. She doesn't just teach success—she embodies it.

For women who are done with the old paradigm of hustle, burnout, and force... Lisa offers something radically different: leadership that feels like freedom.

The Legacy Builder

What sets Lisa Stamper apart isn't just her brilliance—it's her depth.

She doesn't just help her clients make money.

She helps them remember who they are.

Lisa's signature methodology is designed to clear subconscious blocks, activate purpose, and build empires that are rooted in soul, not ego. Her Millionaire Flow Protocol©, for example, fuses energetic alignment with next-level strategic moves that unlock high-cash months without burnout. Her clients don't just hit new income levels—they evolve into leaders who hold more power, peace, and prosperity than ever before.

And the ripple effect is massive. Lisa's community of bold, embodied leaders is creating a new standard of success—one where impact, intuition, and income coexist in harmony. Her work is changing boardrooms, bank accounts, and belief systems across the globe.

But for Lisa, it's never just about business.

"It's about becoming the most fully expressed version of yourself," she says. *"Because when you lead from that place—everything expands."*

Boss Moves in Motion
As we look to the future of leadership, Lisa Stamper stands as a defining voice in the evolution of entrepreneurship.

She's proof that you can lead with heart and still command the room. That you can be spiritual and still dominate your niche. That you can scale your empire and still stay deeply aligned with your truth.

For the women who are ready to rise, to reclaim, and to build something bigger than themselves—Lisa is not just a mentor. She is the movement.

And in the world of boss moves, few are making them as masterfully as Lisa Stamper.

Connect With Lisa

Website: www.lisastamper.com
Facebook:www.facebook.com/lisastamperintuitive
Book: *The Success Codes* – Available now
Community: The Evolve Community

she wins
WOMEN'S NETWORK

SPEAK AT SHE WINS GLOBAL SUMMIT 2025

NOVEMBER 6–7, 2025 | LAS VEGAS, NV

The **She Wins Global Summit 2025** is calling all bold, passionate, and purpose-driven women to take the stage. This powerful **2-day event** will bring together over **500 women leaders, entrepreneurs, and professionals** from around the world for a transformational experience. As a speaker, you'll share your knowledge, story, or expertise in front of a **global audience**—while gaining massive visibility, media exposure, and high-level networking opportunities.

Topics include finance, leadership, business growth, mental health, branding, AI, wellness, innovation, diversity, public speaking, and more. Speaker benefits include a premier speaking slot, TV broadcast of your talk on FENIX TV, media features, red carpet experience, a premium swag bag, gourmet lunch for both days, custom promo graphics, and two full event passes—**valued at over $2,000**, all included with your speaker package.

If you're ready to lead, inspire, and make a real impact, this is your moment. Share your voice, elevate your brand, and join a global movement of unstoppable women.

APPLY NOW

 https://form.jotform.com/250646617740156

OUT OF THE NOISE, INTO PURPOSE:

A MARKETER'S BOLD BREAK FROM BURNOUT

By **Vicky Wu**
CEO, Fractional CMO
Unscrewed Marketing

I was in Paris during the 2015 terrorist attacks. We were a block from the shooting at a café and could hear it. I remember thinking: if something happened to me tonight, what would I regret? Was my legacy really going to be *"overworked"*?

It wasn't about missed vacations or awards or money. My gut-punch was this: I'd spent years climbing the corporate ladder, leading marketing for billion-dollar brands, pushing through 80-hour weeks... and missing years with my kids. This wasn't chasing ambition; I was simply surviving.

That night rewired something in me. I realized I wasn't meant to just do marketing for huge corporations; I was meant to change how entrepreneurs can access it. I wanted to make marketing finally make sense for entrepreneurs. No more cookie-cutter formulas. No more tactics built for big corporations being shoved onto solopreneurs. No more *"just post every day"* advice from people who'd never grown a business themselves.

I'd already worked with tens of thousands of business owners at that point, and I saw the pattern:

they were exhausted, overwhelmed, and Googling their way into circles. 83 million search results and no way to know what advice is legit. Even now with AI, it's just remixing the same old junk, so people still don't know if what they're doing is right or just what's popular but maybe wrong.

That night in Paris made me stop tolerating seeing my entrepreneur friends get bad advice, and stop tolerating the corporate overwork. I left resigned soon after and started helping business owners cut through the noise. I had been helping some entrepreneurs that were associated with the corporation, and now I wanted to help them all. With the right advice. Real strategy. Real context. Real results. No fakexperts. I became obsessed with making marketing feel doable, not dreadful. Human, not hype.

I believe it shouldn't be that hard; marketing should make you feel lighter, not heavier.

I believe busy entrepreneurs deserve better than another regurgitated tip list that may not quite be right for their business.

Today, everything I do is shaped by that moment, because when life gets real, I don't want people to feel lost in the noise. I want them to feel like they finally heard something that actually clicked and that makes their business grow.

That's what lit the fire. And it's still burning.

> **Connect With Vicky**
>
> www.unscrewedmarketing.com
> www.facebook.com/vickywu.us
> www.linkedin.com/company/vickywuguru

Vicky Wu brings 30 years of marketing leadership experience, including CMO and CEO roles, an MBA in Marketing, and a track record with marketing Fortune 500s and multi-billion-dollar brands. Today, she helps small and mid-sized businesses grow with smart, scalable strategies once only available to those big guys with really deep pockets. She's also an author, publisher, ballroom dancer, and artist who enjoys working out in VR.

FROM OVERLOOKED TO ON MISSION

By **Katelyn Rhoades**
Founder, Enfluence Marketing Studio
Host, Call Her Creator

Katelyn Rhoades is a multi-passionate entrepreneur, podcast host, and founder of Enfluence Marketing Studio. After betting on herself and walking away from the 9–5 grind, she built a multi-six-figure business using nothing but social media, storytelling, and a fierce belief that women deserve more than burnout and busywork. Now, through her top-ranked podcast Call Her Creator and digital offers, she empowers women to show up boldly, own their influence, and get paid to do work that lights them up on their own terms.

The moment that lit a fire in me didn't happen in a boardroom or during a big career win. It happened in the quiet chaos of my everyday life, right after my corporate job blindsided me by changing my role without warning.

I had just wrapped up another exhausting day juggling a 9 to 5, motherhood, and freelance work. I was doing everything *"right"* on paper — the job, the clients, the steady paycheck — but deep down, I felt invisible. I wasn't using my voice. I wasn't creating anything that felt like mine. I kept shrinking myself to fit into roles that felt safe, but small.

That quiet realization became the spark.

"What if I stopped waiting to be chosen, and chose myself instead?"

So I did. I started creating content that reflected my real story, not what I thought people wanted to hear. I launched a podcast. I built a brand around helping women grow businesses with social media, strategy, and heart. I showed up consistently, even when the results were slow, even when it felt scary to be fully seen.

Over time, I watched my influence grow, not because I had it all figured out, but because I finally stopped hiding.

That defining moment taught me that the fire we're all looking for doesn't come from accolades or outside validation. It comes from getting honest about what you want, even if it looks different from what everyone else expects of you.

Today, I lead a marketing studio, speak on stages, and coach creators and entrepreneurs to build bold, profitable personal brands. And every time that old fear creeps back in, I remind myself of that moment. The one where I stopped waiting for permission and started becoming who I was meant to be.

Connect With Katelyn

www.enfluencestudio.com
www.instagram.com/thekatelynrhoades
www.podcasts.apple.com/us/podcast/call-her-creator-with-katelyn-rhoades/id1726289174

The SHE RISES STUDIOS
PODCAST

TUNE IN. RISE UP. THRIVE.

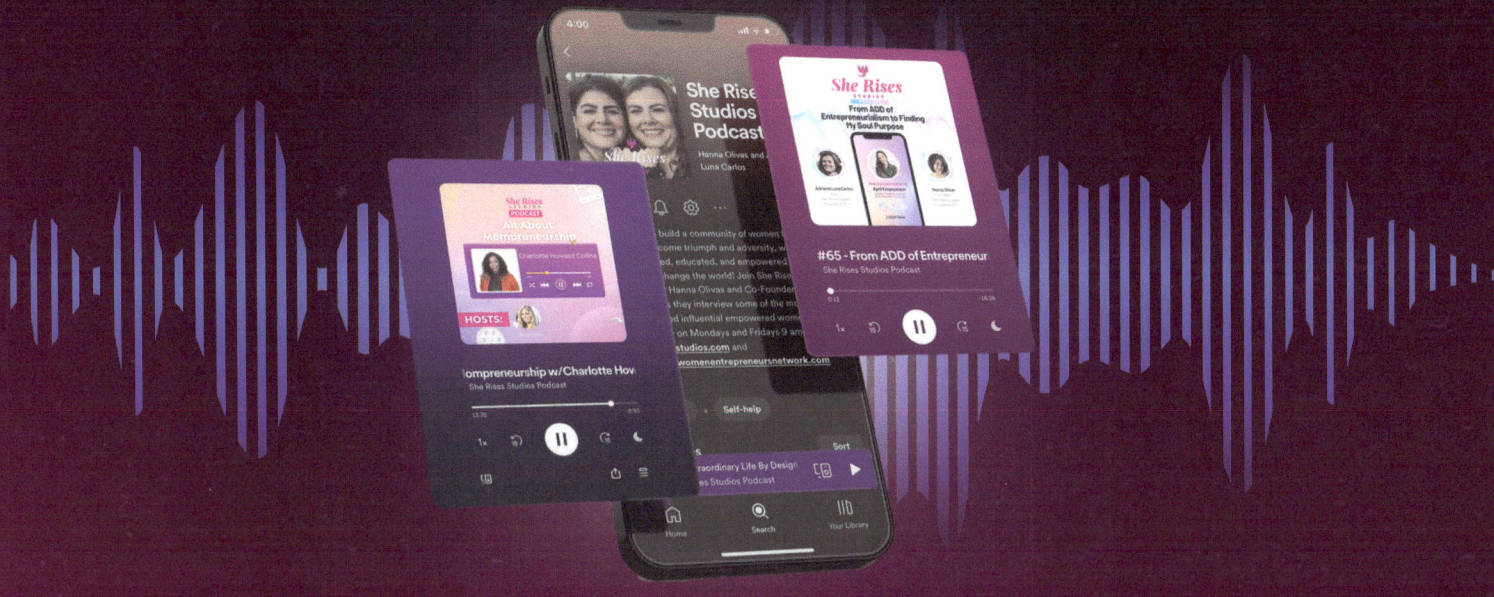

Looking for **real conversations** that inspire, empower, and ignite your potential? The **SRS Podcast** is where women like you come to **learn, grow, and rise!**

Join us for powerful **interviews with trailblazing entrepreneurs, thought leaders, and everyday women** who have turned obstacles into opportunities. Our episodes dive into:

- **Breaking through self-doubt** and stepping into confidence
- **Building a thriving business** with purpose and passion
- **Mastering work-life balance** without guilt
- **Leveling up your mindset, health, and career**
- **Finding your true purpose and living boldly**

Each episode is packed with **real stories, expert insights, and actionable strategies** to help you take your life to the next level. **This isn't just a podcast—it's your roadmap to success!**

SUBSCRIBE NOW AND START YOUR JOURNEY TO EMPOWERMENT!

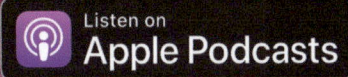 

SHE RISES
STUDIOS

𝒰NLEASH YOUR STORY

BECOME A PUBLISHED AUTHOR!

Have you ever dreamed of sharing your wisdom, experience, or passion with the world? **Now is your time!**

Publishing a book isn't just about writing—it's about **establishing your authority, inspiring others, and creating a lasting legac**y. Plus, with the **$138.5 billion book industry** booming, there's never been a better moment to step into the spotlight.

At **SRS Publishing**, we don't just publish books—we **elevate voices, empower authors, and create change-makers**. Our mission is to help women break barriers, amplify their stories, and thrive in the publishing world. Whether you're an entrepreneur, thought leader, or storyteller at heart, **we're here to guide you every step of the way.**

JOIN THE FASTEST-GROWING PUBLISHING HOUSE FOR WOMEN IN THE USA.

READY TO TURN YOUR DREAM INTO REALITY?

 www.SheRisesStudios.com | *contact@sherisesstudios.com*

GET YOUR COPY NOW

Celebrate the power of women through inspiring stories and insights.

The Unimaginable Journey
Beth MacGowan

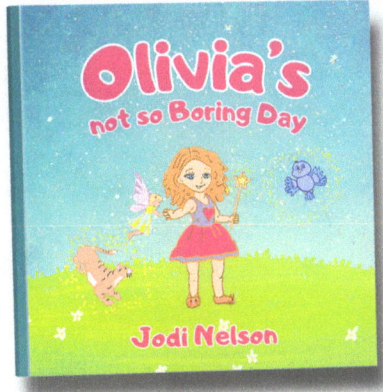

Olivia's Not So Boring Day
Jodi Nelson

Cosmic Butterflies
Tymquana Frierson

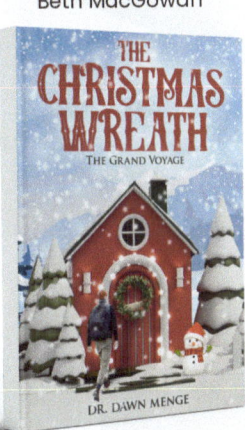

The Christmas Wreath
Dr.Dawn Menge

Dreaming with My Eyes Open
Michela Perry

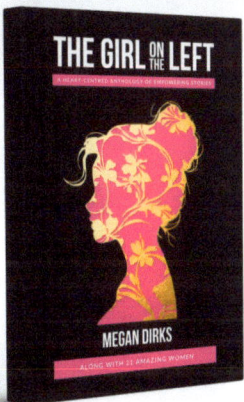

The Girl on the Left
Megan Dirks

A Certain Kind of Sadness
Jillean McClory

Cruz Control
Melissa Cruz

Retreat Within Me
Hoda Jaludi

amazon.com

SHOP NOW

PUBLISHED BY
SHE RISES
STUDIOS